yukismart.com/b/6edad4
AF365387
1
2

baby

nadó

boy

nen

friends

amics

girl

nena

smile

somriure

cry

plorar

hair

cabells

eye

ull

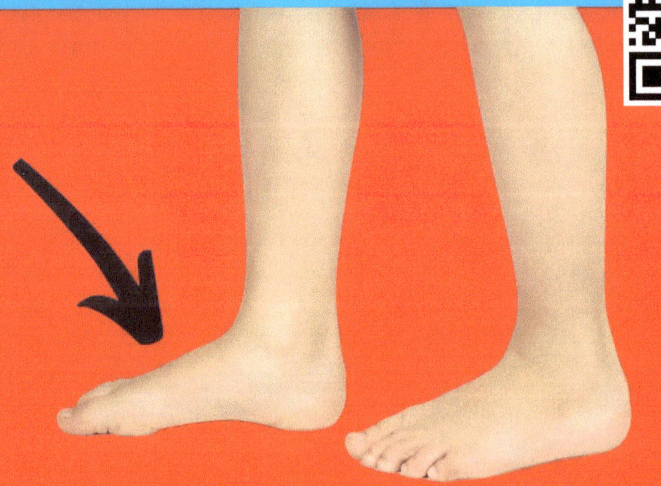

foot

peu

hand

mà

nose

nas

teeth

dents

ear

orella

tongue

llengua

sun

sol

moon

lluna

star

estrella

tree

arbre

bird

ocell

coat

abric

pants

pantalons

dress

vestit

shoes

sabates

red

vermell

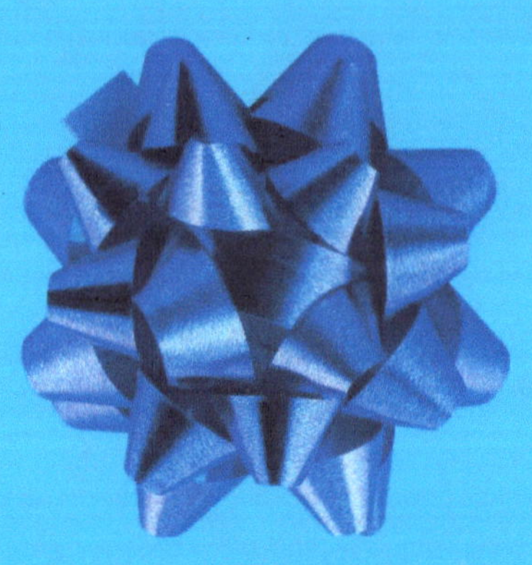

blue

blau

yellow

groc

pink

rosa

white
blanc
green
verd
black
negre

multicolored
multicolor

rainbow

arc de Sant Martí

apple

poma

banana

plàtan

tomato

tomàquet

orange

taronja

carrot

pastanaga

peas

pèsols

potato

patata

corn

blat de moro

lemon

llimona

grapes

raïm

pear

pera

watermelon

síndria

zucchini

carbassó

egg

ou

mushroom

bolet

square

quadrat

circle

cercle

rectangle

rectangle

triangle

triangle

cat

gat

dog

gos

fish

peix

cow

vaca

duck

ànec

chick

pollet

hen

gallina

frog

granota

pig

porc

rabbit

conill

mouse

ratolí

horse

cavall

sheep

ovella

flower

flor

butterfly

papallona

ladybug

marieta

snail

cargol

cake

pastís

bread

pa

clock

rellotge

key

clau

book

llibre

ball

pilota

table

taula

plate

plat

chair

cadira

high chair

trona

fork

forquilla

knife

ganivet

spoon

cullera

cup

tassa

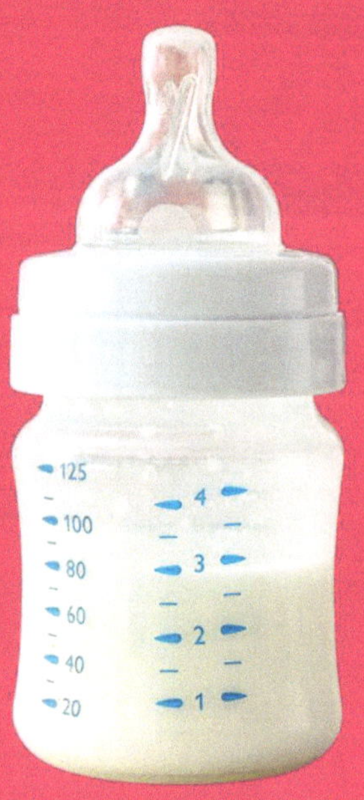

baby bottle

biberó

glass

got

bed

llit

crib

bressol

teddy bear

osset de peluix

pacifier

xumet

towel

tovallola

sink

pica

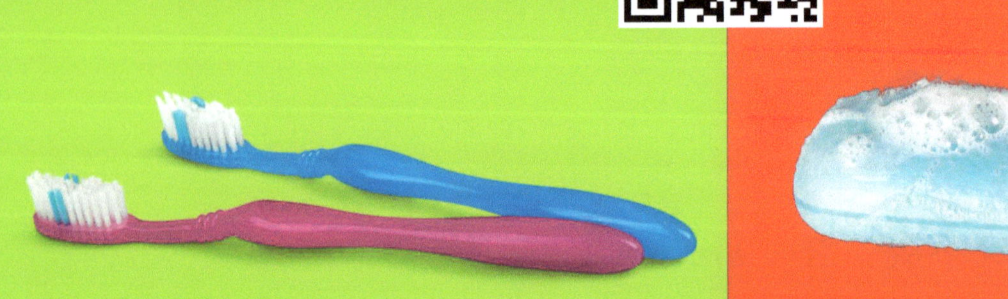

toothbrush

raspall de dents

soap

sabó

toilet

vàter

potty

orinal

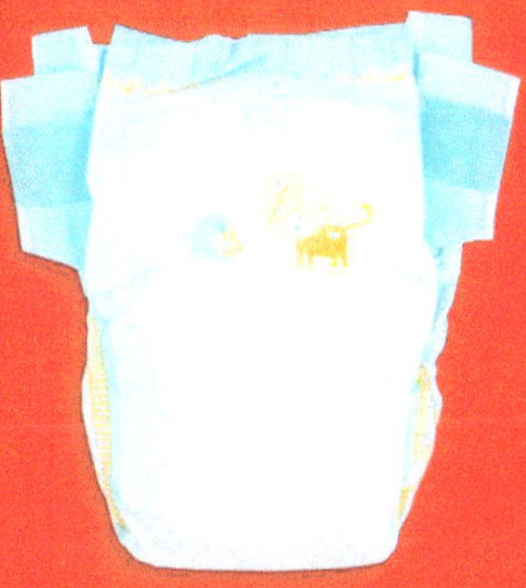

diaper

bolquer

car

cotxe

bike

bicicleta

plane

avió

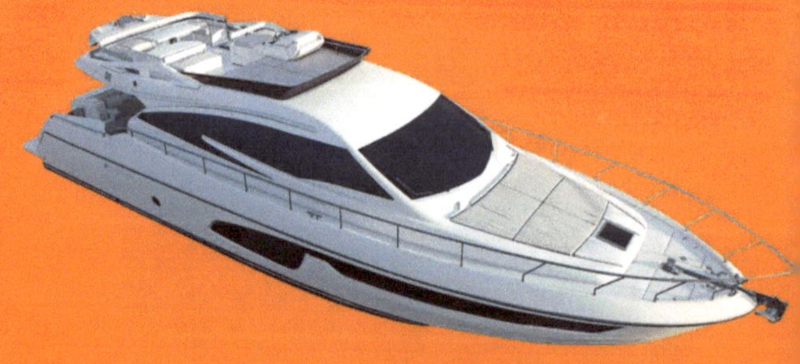

boat

vaixell

firetruck

camió de bombers

train

tren

toys

joguines

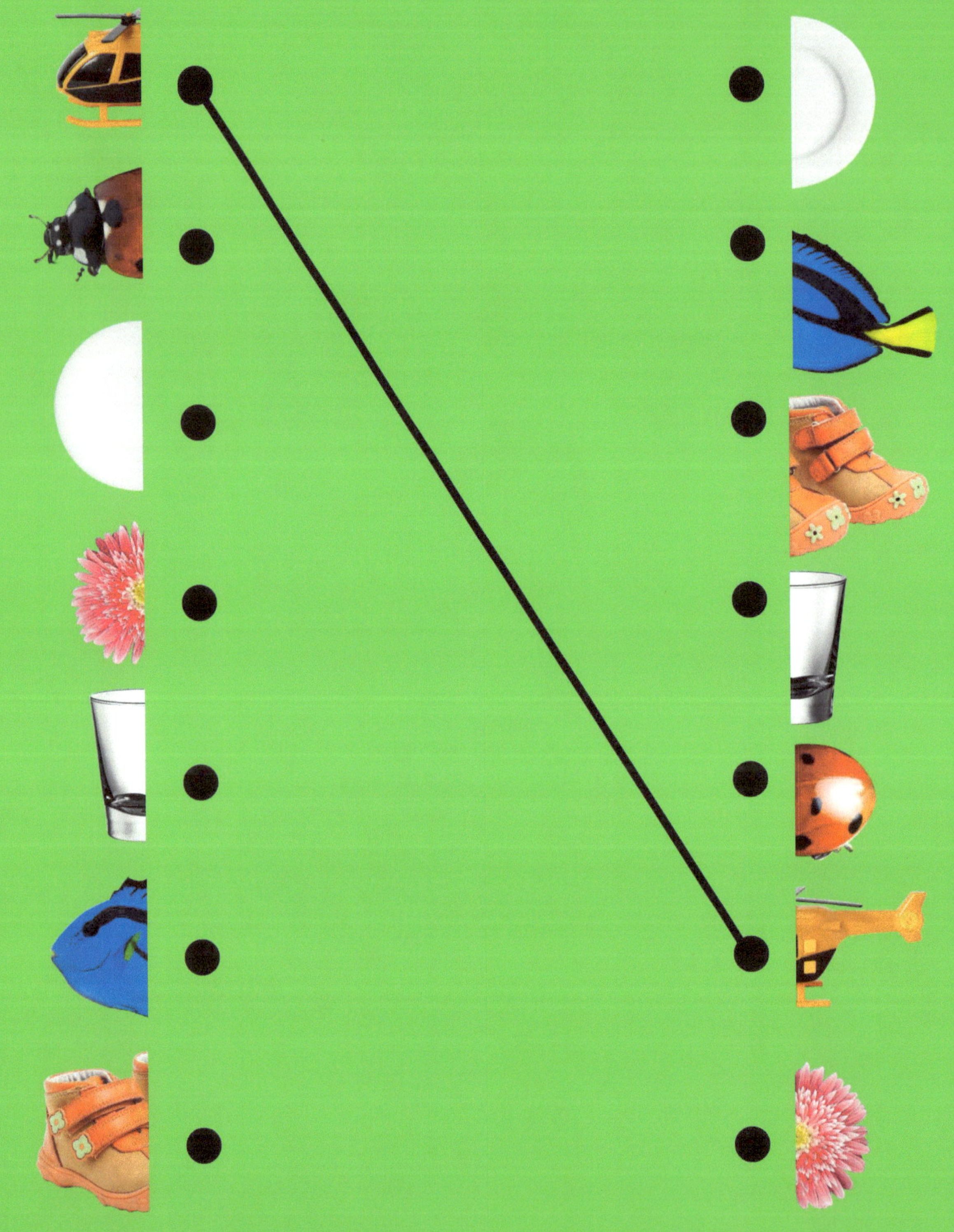